Yogurt
and Cheeses
and Ice Cream
That Pleases

to Miss Gasper, my seventh-grade teacher in Rocky River, Ohio
—B.P.C.

to Dr. Christa Kratz for giving me the opportunity to see the
Milky Way from down here
—M.G.

Milk: A nutritious white liquid produced by mammals. People drink milk from some mammals, such as cows, sheep, and goats. The milk group includes milk and foods made from milk.

Yogurt and Cheeses and Ice Cream That Pleases

What Is in the Milk Group?

by Brian P. Cleary

illustrations by Martin Goneau

consultant Jennifer K. Nelson, Master of Science,
Registered Dietitian, Licensed Dietitian

Cows produce milk in a warm, fluid stream

that later may show up in frozen ice cream!

Or, if the person
in charge of it pleases,

it may end up used
to make hard or soft cheeses.

Milk is produced in a number of mammals, like buffaloes, donkeys, horses, and camels.

But cows, sheep, and goats are the ones that provide most of the **milk** human beings are supplied.

Milk contains calcium— and when we're little

we need it so our teeth and bones
don't turn brittle!

Milk can be served either flavored or white.

Sometimes you stir
till you get it just right!

can help fight diseases, like osteoporosis.

And how about ice cream?
Yes, studies have shown
there's calcium served
in that cup or that cone.

Would you ever think
in your wildest dream

that there's something nutritious
in cookies 'n' cream?

a jug or a bottle
that's filled to the brim

with 2%, 1%,
Whole milk,
or skim.

The milk group contains

things to drink and to eat.

Some are served frozen.

Others, we heat.

Some of these products are spooned; others, sprinkled.

SLUUUURRP!!

Not many food groups are so good for slurping,

22

dunking, and chugging
(which may lead to burping!).

Milk strengthens your teeth,
making two healthy rows.

How much should we have
every day? Take a look—

we've printed a chart
in the back of this book.

Don't "**skim**" too quickly
or else you won't know

a "whole" lot of facts
you can use as you grow!

  =  1 8-ounce carton of milk equals 1 cup

1 slice of Swiss cheese equals 1/2 cup

 =  1 serving (about 1/2 cup) of chocolate pudding equals 1/2 cup

1 8-ounce carton of yogurt equals 1 cup

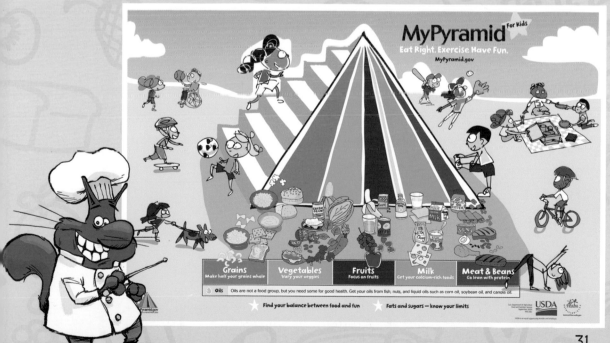

MyPyramid For Kids
Eat Right. Exercise Have Fun.
MyPyramid.gov

Grains	Vegetables	Fruits	Milk	Meat & Beans
Make half your grains whole	Vary your veggies	Focus on fruits	Get your calcium-rich foods	Go lean with protein

Oils Oils are not a food group, but you need some for good health. Get your oils from fish, nuts, and liquid oils such as corn oil, soybean oil, and canola oil.

★ Find your balance between food and fun ★ Fats and sugars — know your limits

This book provides general dietary information for children ages 5–9 in accordance with the MyPyramid guidelines created by the United States Department of Agriculture (USDA). The information in this book is not intended as medical advice. Anyone with food allergies or sensitivities should follow the advice of a physician or other medical professional.

Find activities, games, and more at www.brianpcleary.com

Note to parents and educators: The American Academy of Pediatrics recommends against serving skim and low-fat milk products to children under the age of two unless approved by a pediatrician. Parents and caregivers can gradually begin to introduce low-fat milk products to children ages two to five. After the age of five, low-fat milk products are preferred. Milk-based desserts, such as whole-milk ice cream or yogurt, should be consumed only sparingly as part of a balanced diet.

ABOUT THE AUTHOR, ILLUSTRATOR & CONSULTANT

BRIAN P. CLEARY is the author of the Words Are CATegorical®, Math Is CATegorical®, Adventures in Memory™, Sounds Like Reading®, and Food Is CATegorical™ series, as well as several picture books and poetry books. He lives in Cleveland, Ohio.

MARTIN GONEAU is the illustrator of the Food Is CATegorical™ series. He lives in Trois-Rivières, Québec.

JENNIFER K. NELSON is Director of Clinical Dietetics and Associate Professor in Nutrition at Mayo Clinic in Rochester, Minnesota. She is also a Specialty Medical Editor for nutrition and healthy eating content for MayoClinic.com.

Text copyright © 2011 by Brian P. Cleary
Illustrations copyright © 2011 by Lerner Publishing Group, Inc.

Millbrook Press
A division of Lerner Publishing Group, Inc.
241 First Avenue North
Minneapolis, MN 55401 U.S.A.

Website address: www.lernerbooks.com

Library of Congress Cataloging-in-Publication Data

Cleary, Brian P., 1959–
    Yogurt and cheeses and ice cream that pleases : what is in the milk group? / by Brian P. Cleary ; illustrations by Martin Goneau ; consultant, Jennifer K. Nelson.
        p.   cm. — (Food Is CATegorical)
    ISBN: 978-1-58013-590-0 (lib. bdg. : alk. paper)
    1. Dairy products—Juvenile literature. 2. Dairy products in human nutrition—Juvenile literature. I. Goneau, Martin.
II. Nelson, Jennifer K. III. Title.
    TX377.C54 2011
    641.3'71—dc22   2009049195

Manufactured in the United States of America
1 – PC – 7/15/10